Capital Letters

A B C D E F G

H I J K L M N

O P Q R S T

U V W X Y Z

Lowercase Letters

a b c d e f g h i j k l m n

o p q r s t u v w x y z

Trace and write the letters. Color the picture.

© Carson-Dellosa CD-45

Trace and write the letters. Color the picture.

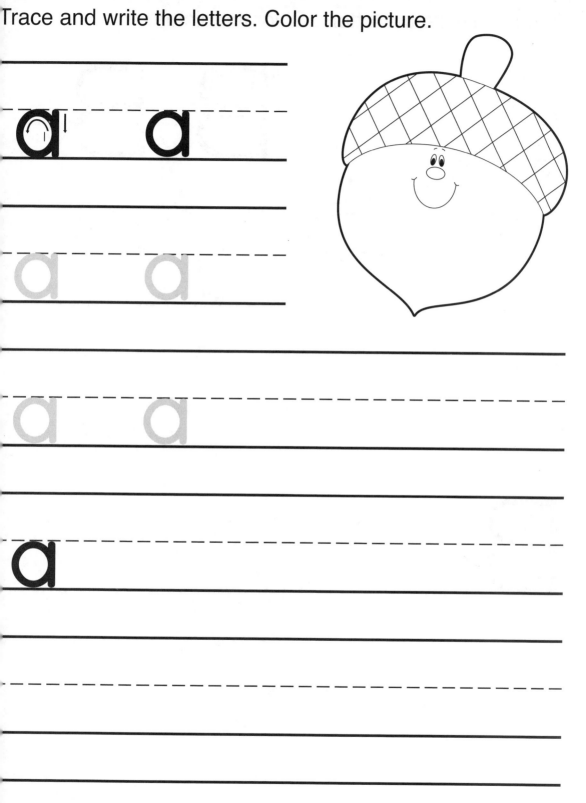

Trace and write the letters. Color the picture.

Trace and write the letters. Color the picture.

Trace and write the letters. Color the picture.

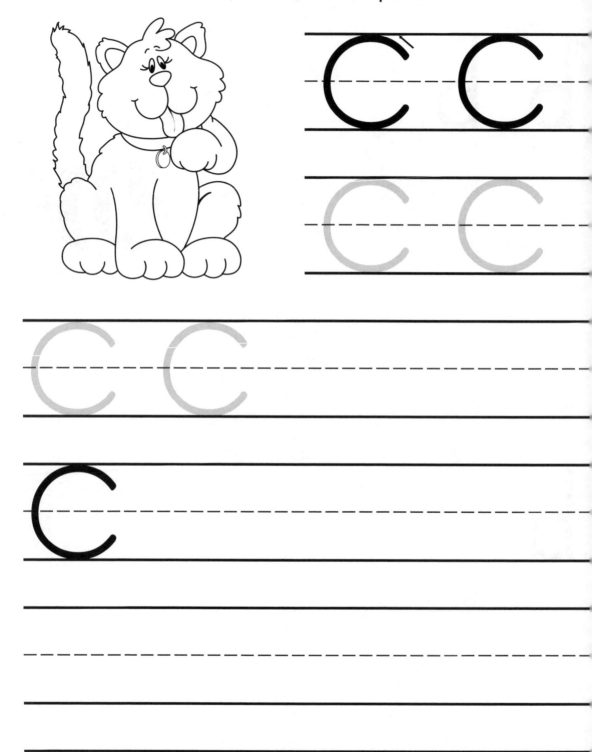

C C

C C

C C

C

Trace and write the letters. Color the picture.

C   C

C   C

C   C

C

Cereal

Trace and write the letters. Color the picture.

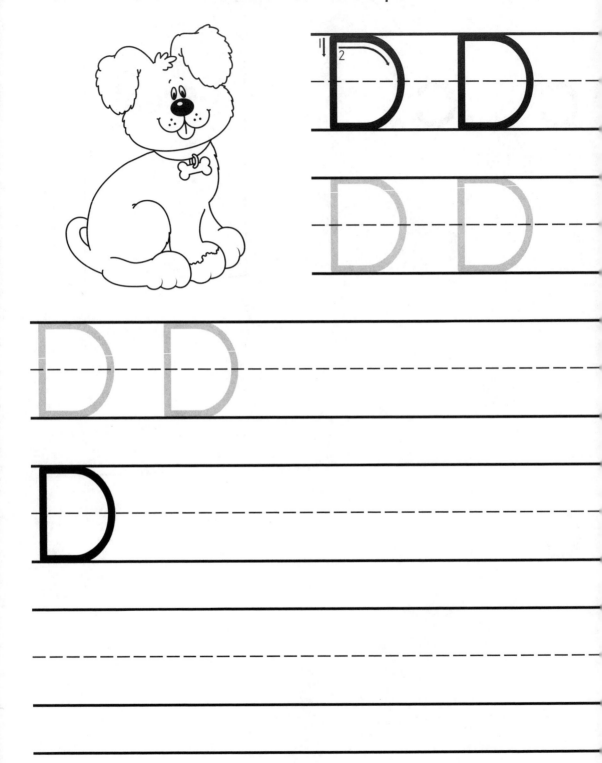

Trace and write the letters. Color the picture.

d d

d d

d d

d

Trace and write the letters. Color the picture.

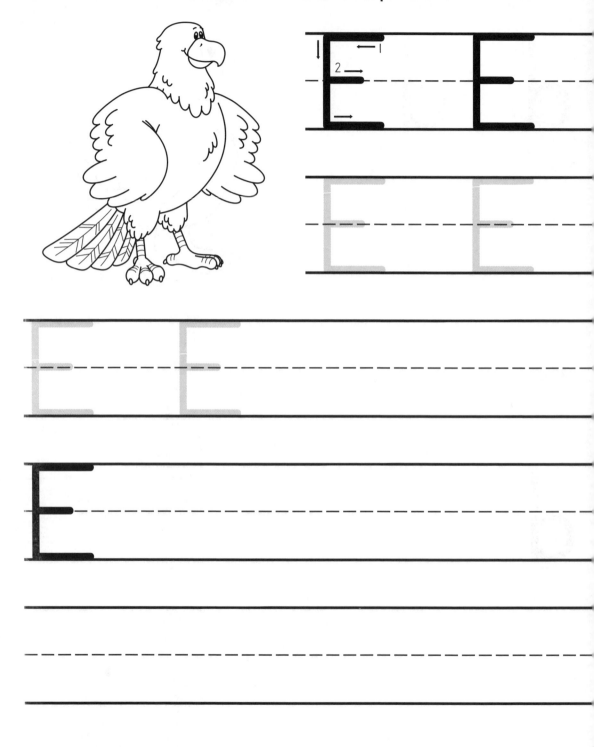

Trace and write the letters. Color the picture.

e   e

e   e

e   e

e

Trace and write the letters. Color the picture.

Trace and write the letters. Color the picture.

Trace and write the letters. Color the picture.

G G G

G G

G G

G

Trace and write the letters. Color the picture.

g g

g

Trace and write the letters. Color the picture.

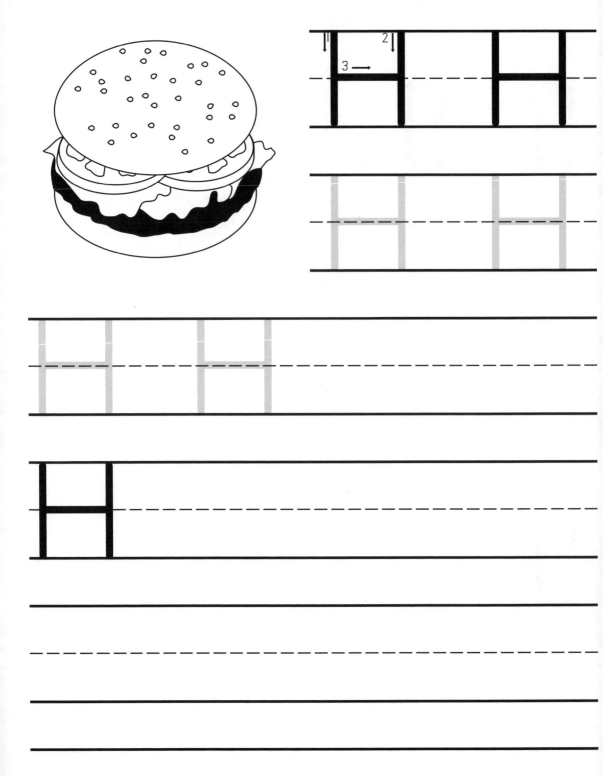

Trace and write the letters. Color the picture.

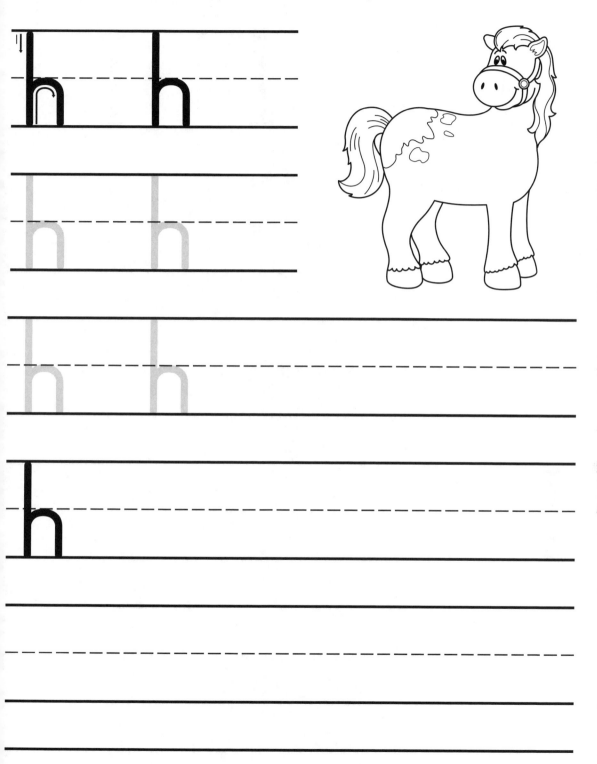

Trace and write the letters. Color the picture.

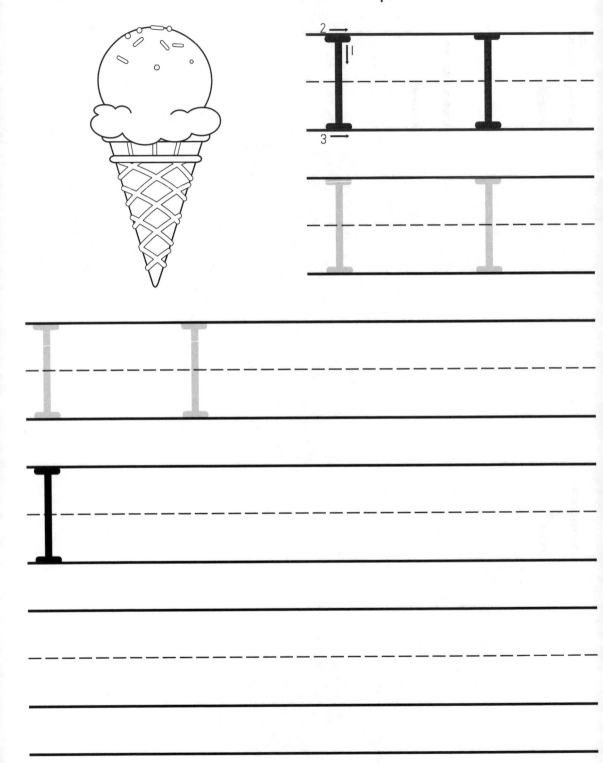

Trace and write the letters. Color the picture.

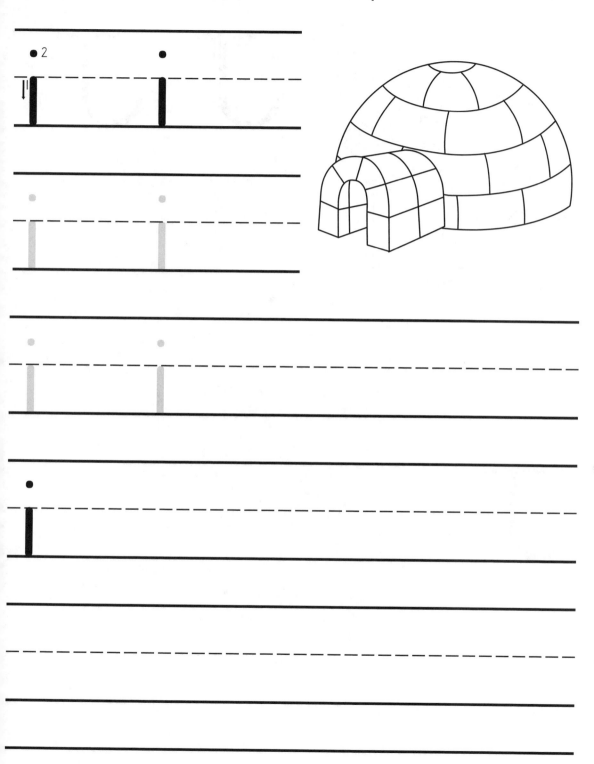

Trace and write the letters. Color the picture.

Trace and write the letters. Color the picture.

Trace and write the letters. Color the picture.

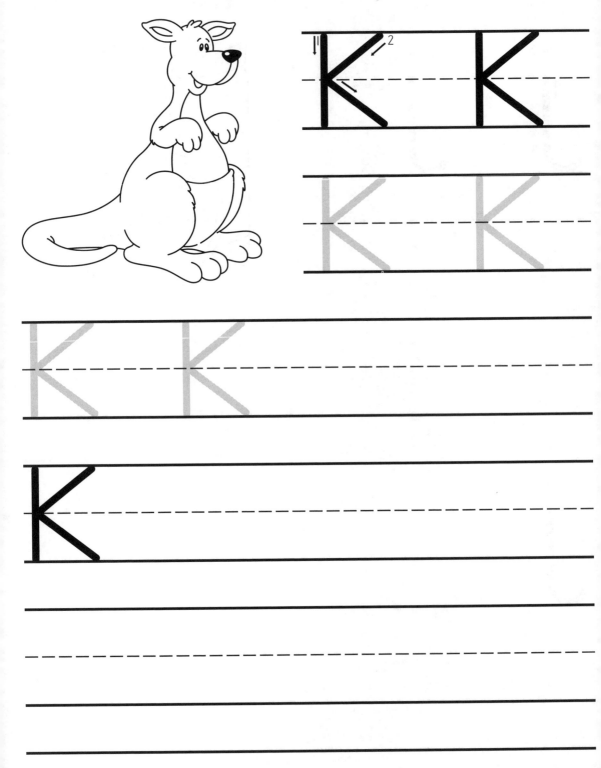

Trace and write the letters. Color the picture.

Trace and write the letters. Color the picture.

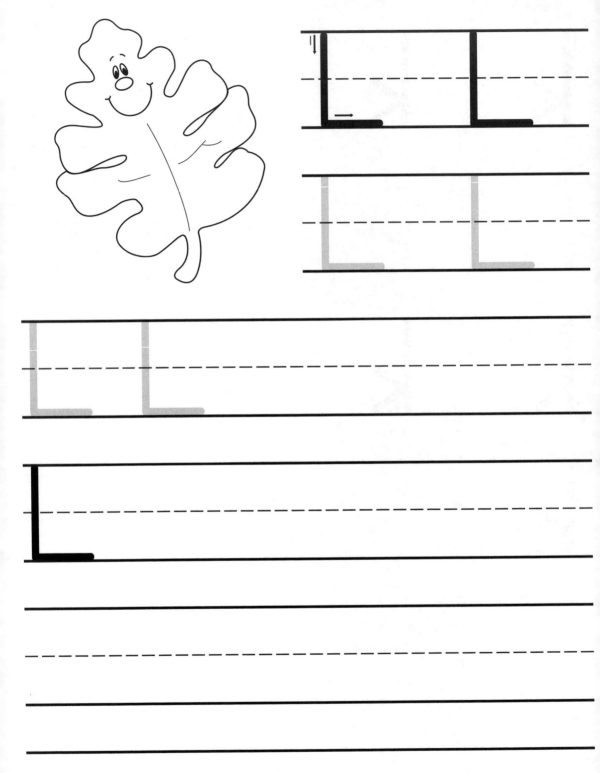

Trace and write the letters. Color the picture.

Trace and write the letters. Color the picture.

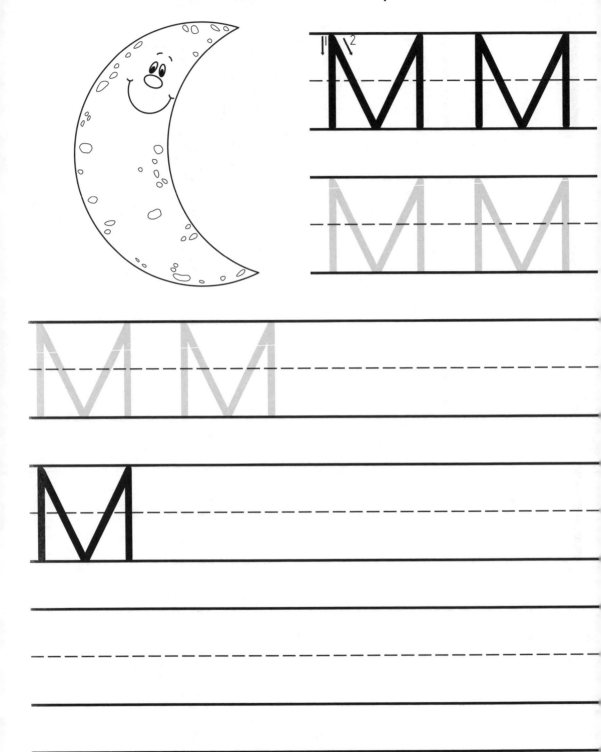

Trace and write the letters. Color the picture.

m m

m m

m m

m

Trace and write the letters. Color the picture.

Trace and write the letters. Color the picture.

n   n

n   n

n   n

n

Trace and write the letters. Color the picture.

Trace and write the letters. Color the picture.

O O

O O

O O

O

Trace and write the letters. Color the picture.

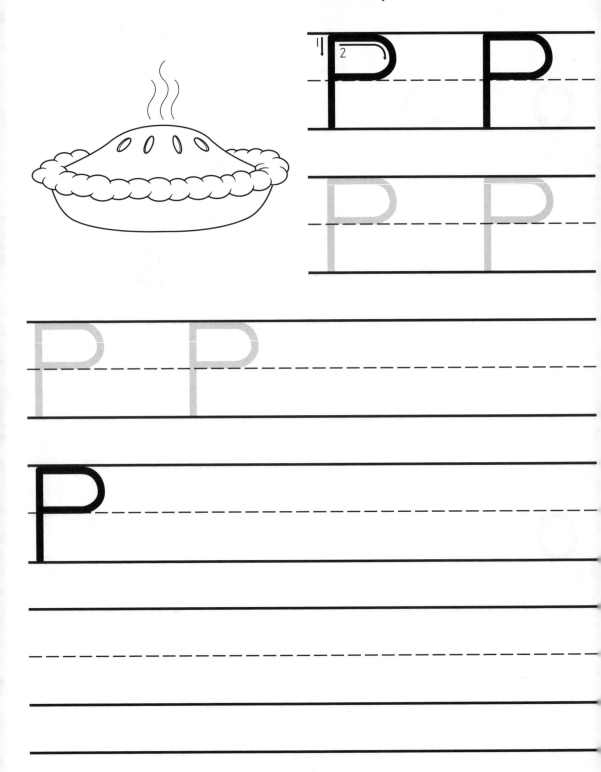

Trace and write the letters. Color the picture.

p   p

p   p

p   p

p

Trace and write the letters. Color the picture.

Trace and write the letters. Color the picture.

q q

q q

q q

q

Trace and write the letters. Color the picture.

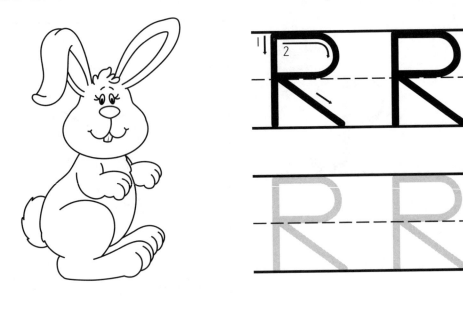

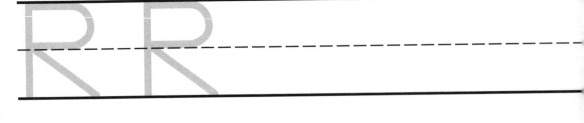

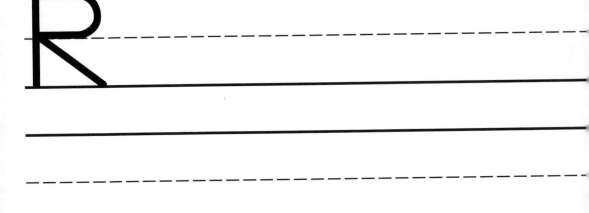

Trace and write the letters. Color the picture.

r   r   r

r   r

r   r

r

Trace and write the letters. Color the picture.

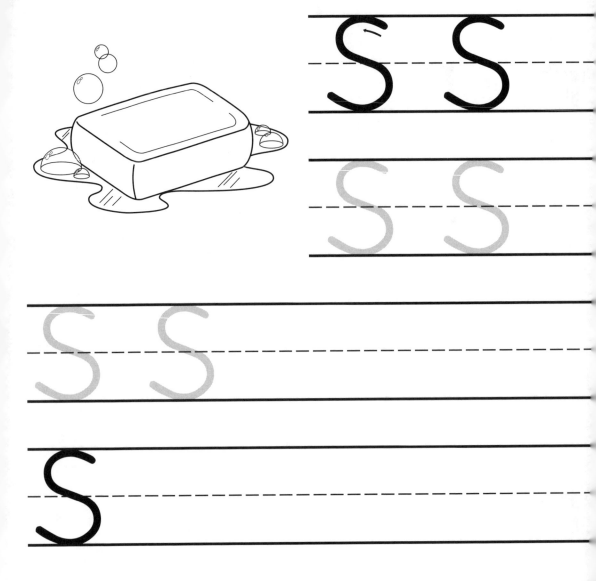

Trace and write the letters. Color the picture.

S S S

S S

S S

S

Trace and write the letters. Color the picture.

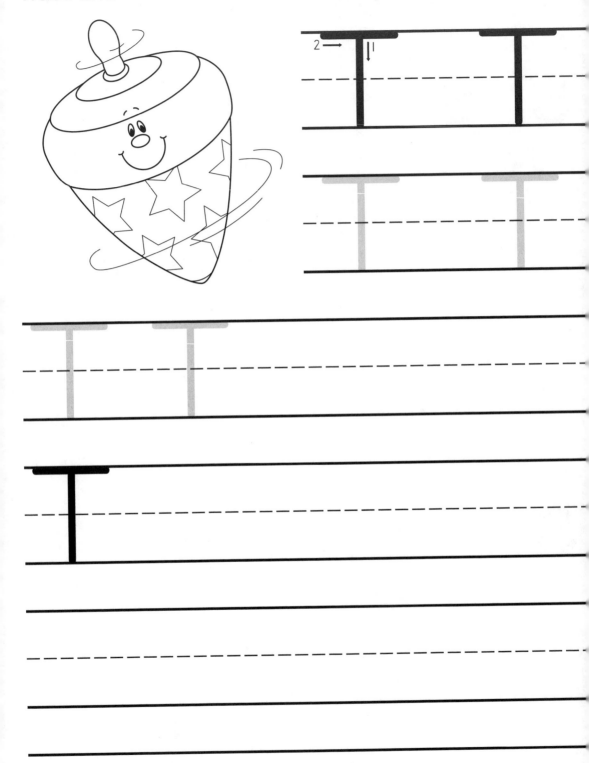

race and write the letters. Color the picture.

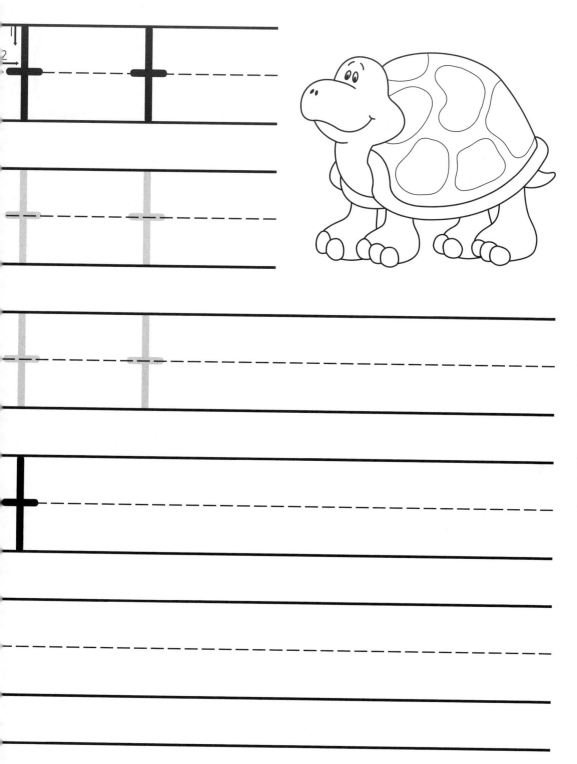

Trace and write the letters. Color the picture.

race and write the letters. Color the picture.

U   U

U   U

U   U

U

Trace and write the letters. Color the picture.

race and write the letters. Color the picture.

V   V

V   V

V   V

V

Trace and write the letters. Color the picture.

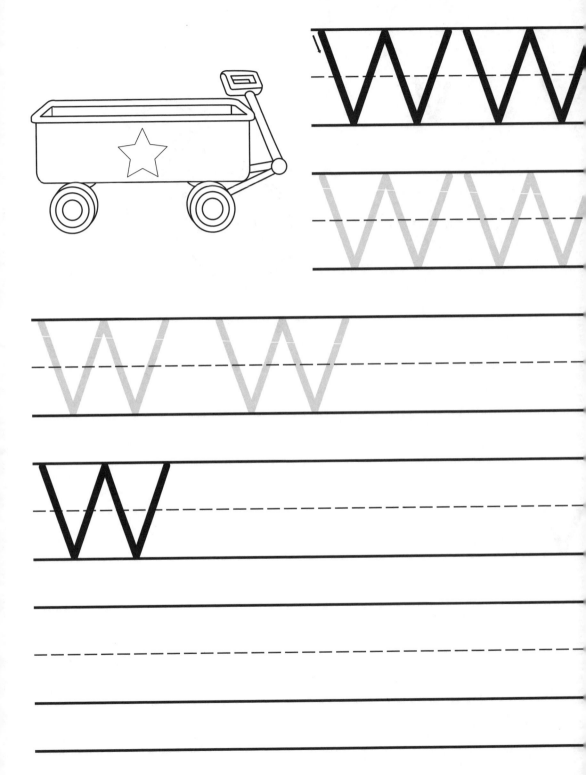

race and write the letters. Color the picture.

W W

W W

W W

W

Trace and write the letters. Color the picture.

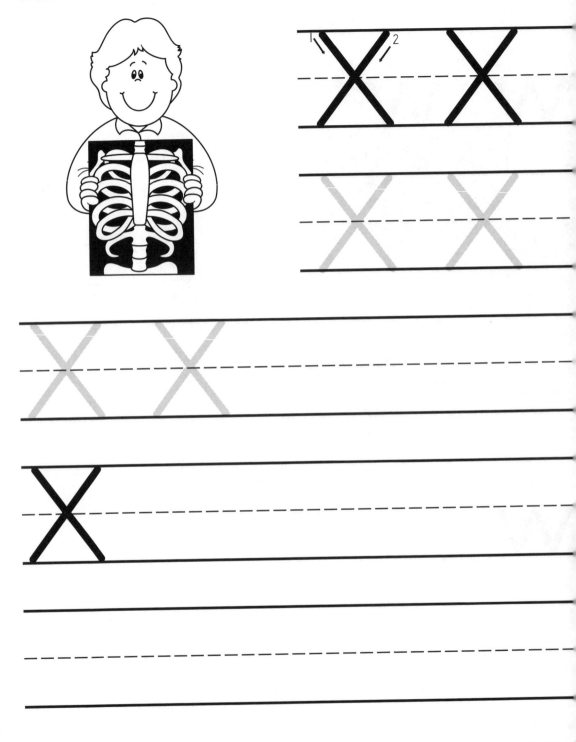

race and write the letters. Color the picture.

X X

X   X

X   X

X

Trace and write the letters. Color the picture.

race and write the letters. Color the picture.

y y   y

y   y

y   y

y

Trace and write the letters. Color the picture.

race and write the letters. Color the picture.

Z Z Z

ZOO

Z Z

Z Z

Z

Draw lines to match the capital and lowercase letters.

M   u

H   v

W   n

V   m

N   h

U   w

Draw lines to match the capital and lowercase letters.

B

P

Q

G

D

R

q

g

p

r

b

d

Draw lines to match the capital and lowercase letters.

Y   z

A   c

O   a

Z   s

C   e

E   y

S   o

Draw lines to match the capital and lowercase letters.

J   x

L   j

X   i

F   k

K   t

I   f

T   l

Write the missing capital or lowercase letters.

A   b

c   D

E   f

G   H

A B C

Write the missing capital or lowercase letters.

i

j

k

L

m

N

O

p

q

R

Write the missing capital or lowercase letters.

S _____ _____ t

U _____ _____ v

W _____ _____ x

_____ y Z _____

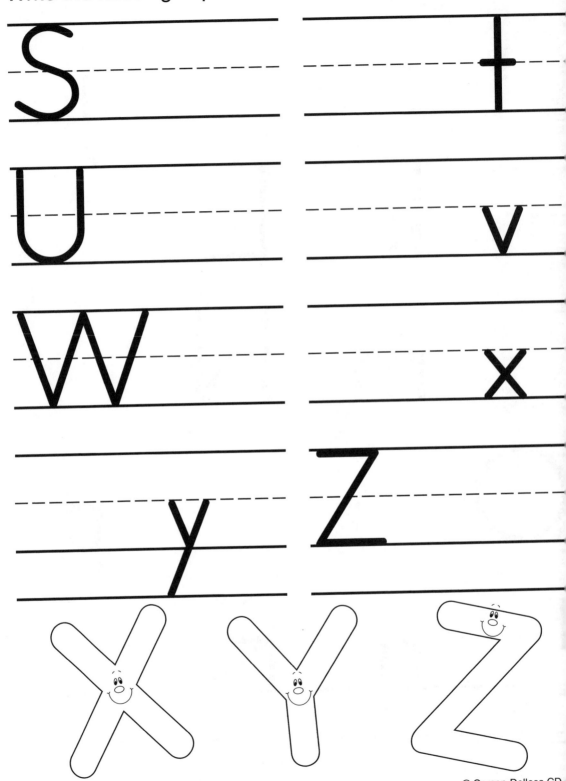

Trace and write the numbers.

0   0

1   1

2   2

3   3

4   4

Trace and write the numbers.

5 5

6 6

7 7

8 8

9 9

Count the objects in each box and write the number.

_____

- - - - - - - - - - - - - - - - - - - -

_____

_____

- - - - - - - - - - - - - - - - - - - -

_____

_____

- - - - - - - - - - - - - - - - - - - -

_____

_____

- - - - - - - - - - - - - - - - - - - -

_____

_____

- - - - - - - - - - - - - - - - - - - -

_____

Count the objects in each box and write the number.

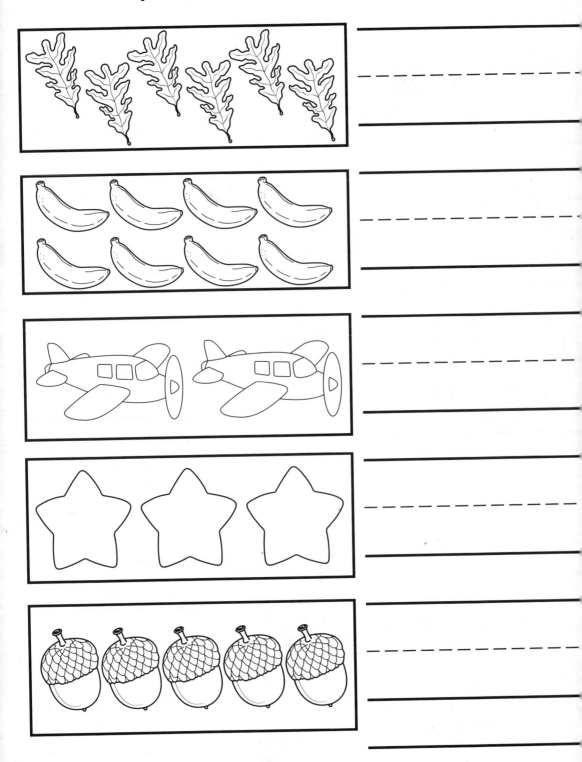
